Valiant Scots

PEOPLE OF THE HIGHLANDS TODAY

North of Scotland Hydro-Electric Board

Valiant Scots

PEOPLE OF THE HIGHLANDS TODAY

by Patricia Lauber

MAPS AND DRAWINGS BY

Donald Pitcher

Coward-McCann, Inc., New York

Library of Congress Catalog Card

Number: 57-7433

Manufactured in the United States of America

VAN REES PRESS • NEW YORK

Contents

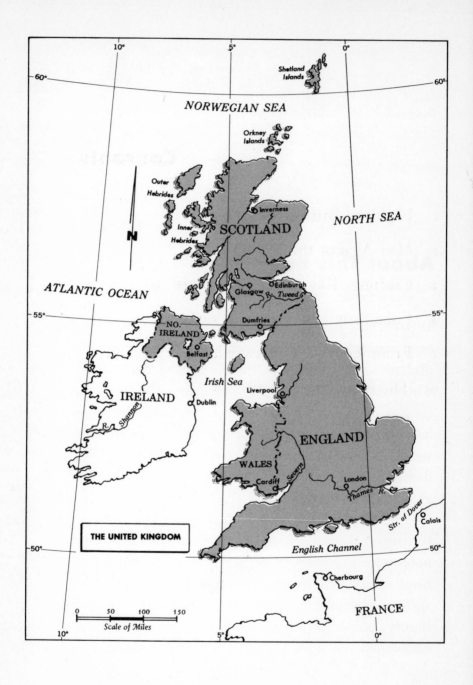

About This Book

WITH SKIRLING BAGPIPES and rattling drums, a Highland band marches through town on a summer evening, the players' kilts swinging to the rhythm of their stride. The band stops to play in the square and then, the concert over, marches out of town and into the green hills beyond. Long after the players have vanished from sight, the pipes can still be heard, a thin wail in the darkening night. Finally even that ghostly sound is swallowed by the hills.

Only then do the listeners break up and move away, for there is a kind of magic to the sound of pipes that holds tourist and townsman alike. To the visitor a pipe band is novelty. To the Highlander it is part of an ancient way of life. Since the beginning of Scottish history, people have danced, married, gone off to war, celebrated, and been buried to the piper's tunes.

Among those tunes, ranging from reels to laments, are many concerning people who have left their Highland home and gone away. "O'er the Isles to America" is one such tune, and its title sums up the others.

That title also sums up a great Highland problem, for the music of a people reflects their way of life. The problem is grave enough to threaten the very existence of Highland life. Yet it can be simply stated:

For 200 years the Highland population has been steadily draining away—o'er the isles to America and many other lands. If the people keep leaving at their present rate, there will be no Highlanders left in another hundred years or so.

This book tells the story behind that problem. It tells of the mighty efforts now being made to solve the problem, to keep the Highlanders from vanishing, like the sound of bagpipes in the hills. The book does not deal with the Scottish Lowlands, where fertile farms, busy mills, shipbuilding yards, and factories support a growing population. It deals only with the mountainous land of northwest Scotland—the Highlands—and with the stubborn, hardy people who cling to that land and try to wrest a living from it.

1. Highland Battleground

IN DAYS GONE BY, the Scottish Highlands were a battle-ground. Warring clans skirmished in the valleys and hunted one another on the mountainsides. Later, Scots and English clashed on Highland soil.

Those wars are long since ended, and today the Highlands look a very peaceful place. Twisting roads climb and drop among green mountains towering against the sky. Sheep graze in hilly pastures. A deer pauses, listening, in the instant before flight, as a dog barks somewhere. In the village below, the people go quietly about their business. A man swings off his bicycle to chat with a friend, then mounts and rides on.

But the appearance is misleading. Today the Highlands are again a battleground. And the war being fought is perhaps the most important in Scottish history. At stake is the very life of the Highlands.

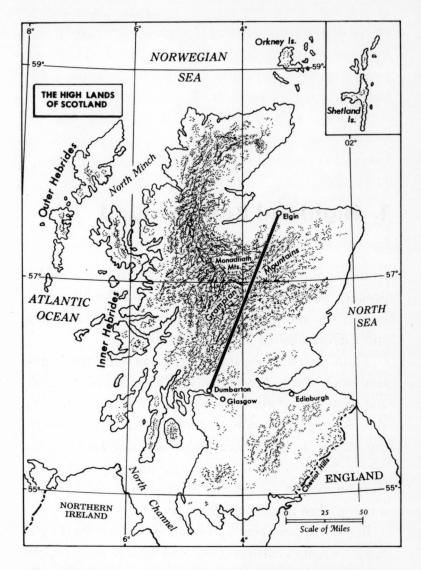

The Highlands are sometimes defined as that part of Scotland lying north and west of a line drawn between Elgin and Dumbarton. Generally speaking, the northwest is the highest—most mountainous —part of Scotland, though the Lowlands are not flat.

The war, which began in the late 1940's, is an attack on the depopulation of the Highlands—the steady draining away of people. In the last 100 years, the Highland population has dropped from 395,000 to 285,000, a decrease of about 25 per cent. The remaining population is top-heavy with old people. It is the young who go away to work and raise their children elsewhere. One village that had 200 school children in 1905 had only 12 by 1955.

The young leave because, in most parts of the Highlands, they cannot earn a decent living. They see no future for themselves or their children. So they go wherever they may find work—the Lowlands, England, the United States, Canada, Australia, and just about any other place you could name.

Yet Highlanders hate to leave home, for theirs is a lovely land of mountains and lakes, valleys and sea. It is greens and purples touched with grays—colors never the same two days running but ever changing under mists or rain or sun. It is a rugged, tranquil land where a man can work all day and hear only the *baa*-ing of sheep or the lowing of cattle, where he sees no movement but the mists and shadows playing on the mountainsides. A traveler may journey for miles in the Highlands and see no town. There will be only villages or lonely little farmhouses dotting the valleys and slopes.

The Highlands are lovely. But think of the scenery in terms of jobs and you come at once to the heart of the

Highland problem. The mountains make transportation
slow and difficult. The landscape is unmarred by sprawl-
ing, smoky factories because there are none. Mountains
and gray outcroppings of rock limit farming. The greens
are more often moss, heather, or a tough, broad fern
called bracken than grassy pastures.

How do the people earn a living?

It doesn't take an expert's eye to see that this is no
farming paradise, yet farming is the largest single occupation in the Highlands. One out of every six Highlanders
is a hard-working farmer who tills a small piece of rented
land. Such farmers are called crofters. Their five or ten
acres of rented farm land is a croft. And their work is
crofting.

The other Highlanders are fishermen, weavers,
shopkeepers, builders, road repairmen, hotel workers,
shepherds. Bring them together for an evening's enter-
tainment, and they become what outsiders expect Highlanders to be—kilted dancers, singers, and bagpipe
players. But by day they are men struggling to wrest a
living from a land that offers little except beauty.

These same men are also the "prize" of the battle now
going on in the Highlands. If they can be helped to earn
a decent living, they will stay home, the drifting away
will cease, and the battle will be won.

The chief weapon in this war is jobs. The Highlanders can be held only if new jobs are created and old
ones improved.

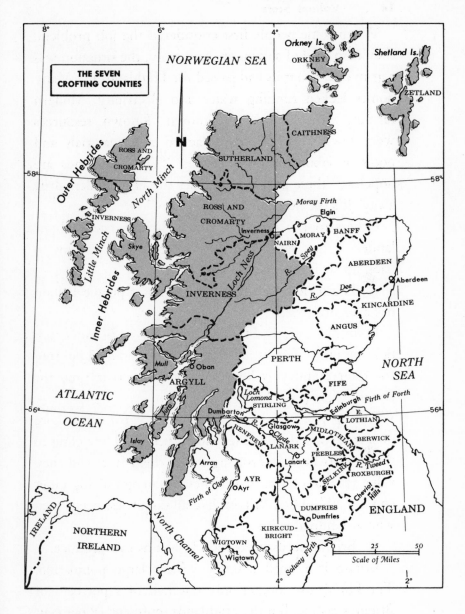

Still another definition of the Highlands is: the seven crofting counties. One out of every six Highlanders is a crofter.

When some people first considered the job problem, they despaired of solving it. And truly, the situation was a grim one. Progress had passed the Highlands by. Many homes lacked running water and electricity. Modern farming methods were unknown. Known resources were few. The Highlands lacked raw materials and pools of labor for big factories. "The Highlands are hopeless," these people said. "Let the Highlanders drift away. It's the best thing they can do."

Others took a different view. "Britain needs Highlanders," they said. And they offered these reasons to back up their opinion:

1. Highlanders are some of the finest people Britain has ever produced.

In time of war, the Highlands have given Britain crack fighting units. The list of Highlanders who died fighting for their country is long indeed. Now it is time for Britain to help the Highlands.

During peacetime, Highlanders have formed a core of sturdy, proud, and independent people. They cling to their crofts because crofting leaves them free; and they value freedom more than riches. In an age of big cities and assembly lines, Britain, like all countries, needs men who are individualists.

2. Britain needs what the Highlands can produce.

Britain is a small country with a large population. The Highlands contain only one half of 1 per cent of Britain's people. But the Highlands represent 18 per cent

18% OF THE LAND AREA . . .

THE HIGHLANDS

SCOTLAND

BUT ONLY

½ OF **ONE** PERCENT

OF THE PEOPLE

ENGLAND

WALES

HIGHLANDS   SCOTLAND   BRITAIN

of Britain's land. That's too big an area to let go to waste. The Highlands could produce food and timber Britain must now buy from other countries.

For these reasons a many-pronged attack was launched to save the Highlands. The men leading the attack are a mixed group. They range from heads of government agencies to private citizens who have seen the chance to help the Highlands and done so on their own. These men sometimes disagree about what should be done or how to do it. But all are working to create jobs and to make old ones better.

Nobody, of course, can create jobs from thin air. They must grow out of what the land offers. So the first big step was to assess the Highlands—to see what they needed, what they had, and what could be done with it.

Out of this survey came a general battle plan: Make the crofts bigger and more fertile. Plant forests. Experiment with tiny factories. Search for resources. Help farmers and fishermen get their produce to market. Lay pipes for running water. Harness Highland streams to produce electricity.

That plan is still being followed. Parts of it have gone very well. Others are lagging. And so it is not yet clear whether or not the battle will be won.

The task ahead is still tremendous. The men who have shouldered it face a double problem: They must build for the future and at the same time undo the damage of the past. For it was other men who, long ago, stripped the Highlands of their wealth and started the people on the road to exile.

2. Man Against the Land

DURING THE 1600's, the Highlands were the wildest part of Britain. In name only were they ruled by the parliament that sat in Edinburgh. The true rulers were the Scottish chiefs.

The chiefs—MacDonalds, MacKenzies, MacLeods, Campbells, and scores of others—held large areas of land. Each ruled his land and the clansmen who lived on it. The wild and lawless chiefs were mighty hunters and mighty warriors. Their favorite sport was invading the lands of other chiefs to steal sheep or long-haired Highland cattle. From time to time they carried these raids southward into the Lowlands.

For raids—or defense—a chief called up his clansmen. The clansmen, living on the chief's land under his protection, farmed small patches of ground to produce their food. The men wore kilts of the chief's tartan and the women wore dresses spun and woven from the wool of family sheep. The clansmen paid their rent not with cash but military service to the chief. A fiery cross was carried around to summon them in times of need.

At that time the main industry in the Highlands was cattle raising. The cattle were driven south over trails, called drove roads, and sold in Lowland markets. Cattle on the trail were so likely to be raided that an adventurous young man named Rob Roy made a fine business out of guaranteeing them against theft. If cattle under his protection were raided, he replaced them with others stolen from clans that had not bought his protection.

The chiefs ruled unthreatened by southern law because of the land itself. Mountains dominating valleys and moors, and islands guarding harbors, were natural strongholds. Almost the only roads were cattle trails, and communities were isolated from one another. The

Ancient castle, still standing, guards a water approach.

British Travel Association

people were untamed by law, and the countryside was untamed by man. The way of life was primitive, but it developed a hardy, courageous people. Still more important, it was the established way of life, one that fitted land and people, despite its many drawbacks.

In time this way of life would have had to change. Had it changed gradually and from within, Highland problems today might be easier to remedy. But the changes came from outside. In the late 1600's a chain of events began which were to strip the Highlands of their natural wealth, destroy the established way of life, and start the waves of emigration that have continued to this day.

1. The Darien Company

In the year 1695, Scotland and England had the same king, but in all other ways they were two separate countries. Each had its own parliament and laws. Each was building up its own foreign trade. In fact, Scotland's foreign sales of leather and woolen goods were doing so well that English merchants became alarmed. Fearing that Scotland's trade might cut into their own, they had Scottish goods banned in all English colonies and in all countries with which England had treaties.

The Scots answered with a daring plan of their own. They decided to start a Scottish colony at Darien (Panama). They would make it a free port, open to all nations, where goods could be traded without payment of duty. Darien would become a giant clearinghouse for Scottish goods.

To carry out this plan, leading Scots formed the Darien Company. In every part of Scotland, people's savings were invested in the company. The company bought a fleet of 35 ships, equipped them, and loaded them with settlers and goods.

The 35 ships crossed the Atlantic without difficulty, but when the settlers tried to land at Darien, they found themselves facing Spanish troops. English merchants had persuaded Spain to prevent the landing.

The settlers moved to another site. Here they were attacked by yellow fever. Many died, and the others realized they could not colonize such an unhealthy place. Joined by a second fleet that had arrived from Scotland, they sailed north, first to Jamaica and then to New York. At both places English governors refused to let the fleet take on food or water for the voyage home. Only a few of the would-be settlers lived to reach Scotland.

The failure of the Darien plan ended Scottish hopes for a free port. It brought complete poverty to the country. Money makes the wheels of business go round. Scotland had lost most of its capital.

Purchasing power in the Lowlands was destroyed. This, in turn, destroyed cattle raising, the main industry of the Highlands. If the Lowlands couldn't buy cattle, the Highlands couldn't sell them.

2. The Rebellions

The Scottish rebellions of 1715 and 1745 are famous in song and story. They are usually described as attempts to put a Stuart—a descendant of Mary, Queen of Scots—back on the throne. But there is more to the story than that. The truth is that well-fed, prosperous people seldom rebel. In the two Scottish rebellions, hunger and poverty played a large part in stirring up the people.

The 1715 rebellion was short-lived, but the '45 rebellion came close to succeeding. It's the one that makes exciting reading, with tales of Bonnie Prince Charlie sailing from France to land in the islands of the Outer Hebrides, hiding in caves, leading the clansmen in battle, marching on London, and escaping to Skye disguised as Flora MacDonald's maid. Some historians think that if Charles had pressed on to London instead of being persuaded to turn back, he might have won the day.

Glenfinnan monument to Prince Charlie.

British Travel Association

Both rebellions brought forth the same kind of punishment. The victorious English set out to break up the clan system and to punish chiefs who had rallied round the Stuart banner.

Many of these chiefs had their heads cut off. All lost their estates. The English seized the lands and put them up for auction. Until 1782 the wearing of the kilt and the playing of bagpipes were forbidden.

Selling the estates ended the old relationship between clansman and chief. It created a new one of crofter (or tenant farmer) and landlord. A few landlords treated the crofters fairly. Most demanded a higher rent than a croft could afford. This started the first great wave of emigration. Many crofters packed up and left for other lands. Those who stayed struggled to improve their land and houses. Landlords, seeing the improvements, promptly raised the rent. Since a crofter had no lease, he had no protection. The owner was free to put him off the land without even paying for improvements made by the crofter. Emigration continued.

In 1785, chiefs were offered the chance to buy back their lands. Many did so, but to raise the money they had to tax their own clansmen living on the land. This again caused a large wave of emigration, mainly to North America. It was during this period that the Carolinas gained a large Scottish population.

To bring the Highlands under control, the English had built military roads. Large companies from the

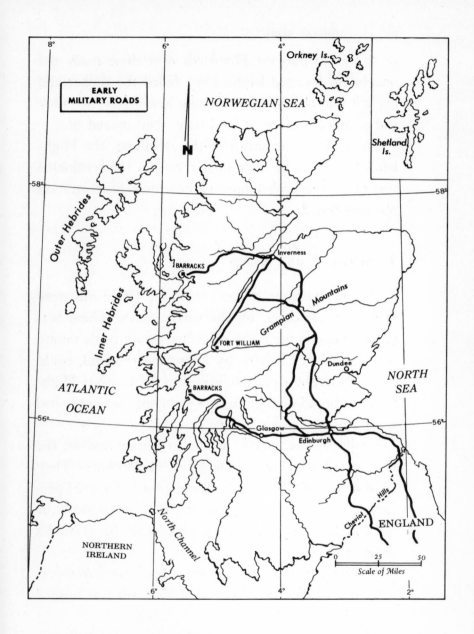

Military roads were the first to penetrate the Highlands.

south moved into the Highlands over these roads and bought up forested lands. They felled the timber and made it into charcoal for smelting iron ore. When they had stripped a piece of land bare, they moved on.

Thus, in the aftermath of the rebellions, the Highlands lost much of their timber wealth; the traditional way of life was broken up; and the pattern of emigration was established.

3. Seaweed and Sheep

Despite the blows of the 1700's, the Highlands were making a comeback by the early 1800's. There was money again in the Lowlands. That meant cattle raising was profitable. Crofters, by improving the land, could feed and clothe their families. And in the west Highlands a brand-new industry—gathering seaweed—had sprung up to meet a change in taste.

Until the late 1700's, people in Britain and on the Continent hadn't bothered much about cleanliness. They seldom washed. Those who could afford it poured perfume over themselves instead. Then, quite suddenly, it became the fashion to wash oneself. And this created a demand for soap.

A chief ingredient of the soap was sodium carbonate, or soda ash. The main source of soda ash was burned seaweed.

The Scottish west coast was rocky and heavily indented. Every storm blew huge masses of seaweed into hundreds of little bays and inlets. As coastal Highlanders gathered and burned seaweed, their villages found a new prosperity and whole families came to depend on seaweed for their living.

Then a chemist discovered a way to get sodium carbonate from salt. In London, lawmakers took the tax off salt, making it cheaper to produce soap from salt than from seaweed. Overnight the seaweed industry collapsed and vanished like a soap bubble.

At the same time that washing became fashionable, a still bigger change was taking place. This was the Industrial Revolution. The machine age had arrived in Britain.

In England and the Scottish Lowlands, factories were being built apace. Many of these were mechanized power mills for making woolen goods. The mills ate up bale after bale of wool. And this brought about the most drastic change in the Highlands yet, the clearances.

Owners of large Highland estates—some English, some Scots—decided there was far more money to be made from raising sheep for wool than from renting land to crofters. Since the crofters were farming the most fertile areas, the estate owners simply cleared them off the land.

Whole villages were uprooted from fertile land. The people were sent to live along the coast or on barren, stony hillsides where even sheep could not graze. Some

Stones mark foundation of house leveled during clearances.

crofters decided to leave the country, and sailed for Canada and the United States. Others, who refused to move, were hurled aboard ships and sent off to the New World without a penny to their names or any possessions save what they had on their backs.

The clearances went on until the 1880's, when public opinion was finally aroused and an investigation made. In 1886, a law was passed to protect crofters. Under this law, crofters (or their descendants) could not be put off the land so long as they paid their rent.

The new law stopped the clearances, but the damage was done.

Thousands of acres of fertile farm land had been turned over to sheep. The number of acres under plow dropped from 800,000 in 1800 to 70,000 in 1885.

Cattle raising suffered a similar fate. In 1800, 356,000 head of cattle grazed in the Highlands. By 1885 this number was down to 95,000.

Worst of all, tens of thousands of strong, young Highlanders had been forced out of their native land.

A Summing Up

No matter what had happened in England and the rest of the world, Highland life would have undergone vast changes in the 1700's and 1800's.

The clan system could not have continued into modern times.

Some Highlanders would have had to leave home, for the Highlands could not support a large population with modern standards of living. In the old days, people were content to live quietly on a small piece of land, eating and wearing what they could raise. Today people ask more of life. A small farm cannot supply all their wants.

The trouble was that changes were brutally enforced with no thought given to their effect on the Highlands' future. The clan system was smashed, but nothing else was substituted for it. Timber wealth was stripped away. The most fertile land was given over to sheep, with crofters left to farm the barren land. Old industries disappeared from the Highlands, but no new ones came to take their place. Uncontrolled emigration drained away much of the young blood.

Man-made damage in the Highlands was so great that the trend continued even when the clearances ended. Between 1885 and 1954, the number of acres being

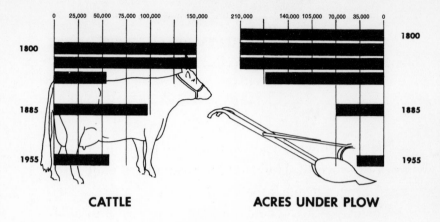

0	25,000	50,000	75,000	100,000		150,000

210,000		140,000	105,000	70,000	35,000	0

1800

1885

1955

1800

1885

1955

CATTLE　　　　　　　**ACRES UNDER PLOW**

British Travel Association

Chart shows decrease in Highland cattle raising and farming.

farmed fell from 70,000 to 38,000, the number of cattle from 95,000 to 58,000. A hundred years ago, 18 per cent of the Scottish population lived in the Highlands. Today 6 per cent lives there. The population of Scotland as a whole is increasing. The population of the Highlands is decreasing.

Only in the late 1940's was a vigorous attack launched on Highland problems. Its aim was to stem the drifting away of the Highland people. Its weapon was jobs.

A large part of the attack has been aimed at improving crofting. For Highland crofting is not just a means of earning a living. It is the basic way of life.

British Travel Association

Amid Highland beauty the people struggle to earn a living.

3. Crofting: Key to the Highlands

A LONELY CROFT HOUSE, snuggling against a hill for shelter, is almost invisible. Its gray walls blend into gray rock and the dark greens of the land so that only a column of blue smoke rising from the chimney catches the eye and signifies this is a home.

The smoke has an odd, heavy, biting odor that is the smell of burning peat. Peat is the crofter's fuel, which he digs himself and pays for only with his labor.

Peat, the first cousin of coal, is decayed vegetable matter that builds up in wet areas, and there are many peat bogs in the Highlands. A crofter in search of fuel digs a shallow trench in the bog and cuts the peat into brick-shaped pieces. He leaves them on the ground to dry and, at the summer's end, carries them home to stack by the door of his house.

If the croft house is an old one, its walls are made

Whitewashed stone croft house snuggles into hillside on Skye.

of gray stone gathered from the land by the crofter or perhaps his father. Each wall is double. The space between, packed with dirt, sand, or pebbles, makes the house wind-proof in winter. The roof is chunks of turf braced on rafters and thatched with straw so that it will shed rain. A network of ropes weighted with stones holds the thatched roof in place during winter storms, while the rounded corners of the house allow the winds to slide by. Inside, the floor is beaten earth. The two or three rooms are furnished with wooden chairs, a table, and bunklike beds built into the walls. Almost everything that went into the making of this house came from the land about.

In many places, old croft houses are being replaced with new, which look like stone or concrete houses anywhere. These square, small houses are divided into four rooms with wooden floors and plenty of windows.

If the family is home, a stranger is sure to be invited in and offered tea. Highlanders are famed for their open-handed hospitality and would not think of letting a stranger go before he had shared in whatever the house could offer. This trait often comes as a surprise to people who have known Scotch jokes without knowing the Scots. The truth is that the jokes were invented by the Scots themselves. Since most Scots are extremely generous, a tight-fisted man became the butt of village jokes.

The same sort of wry humor lies behind much of what the crofter says. He's a plain-spoken man and can

New croft house stands beside old now used for animals.

Lauber

talk on almost any subject, for he is widely read and well informed. Education is highly prized in Scotland and reading is a major pastime during the long winters. Although the warm currents of the Gulf Stream keep Scotland's climate mild, the Highlands lie as far north as Hudson Bay in Canada. Winter days are short. During the long nights, when outdoor work is impossible, the people read. The crofter may also be a traveled man. If he lives near the coast, he has probably served in the merchant marine, visited North America, and perhaps even worked in the United States for a few years.

Nevertheless, he has returned to spend his life tilling a few acres of potatoes, barley or oats; hay if he has a cow to feed during the winter. Chickens and a few sheep complete the list of his possessions. Most of his work is done by hand, and it pays badly. Still, this is the way of life the crofter has chosen because it leaves him free. He sets his own hours and works to please only himself. Like farmers everywhere, he loves his land and the independence it gives him.

That, interestingly enough, was the strongest argument put forth for crofting as a way of life by a group of hardheaded experts. Appointed by the government to study Highland crofting, they made a long report suggesting ways that crofting could be improved. Time and again they made the point that Britain needs crofting because it is a "free and independent way of life."

Lauber

Roddy Matheson stands with his father on their Skye croft.

One of the first things to be done, said the experts of the Crofting Commission, is to make the crofts bigger. The crofters themselves say the same thing.

Just outside Portree, on the island of Skye, there's a croft farmed by the Matheson family. Roddy, the son living at home, does most of the work because his father is nearly blind. But since a croft can't support the family, Roddy also works full time as the postman in Portree. At first glance, Roddy pedaling his bike in a postman's uniform bears little resemblance to the kilted Highland warriors who were his ancestors. But he shares with them a sturdy, stubborn courage. The ancient clansmen applied it to fighting. Roddy applies it to the long, hard job of farming poor land. Slowly and laboriously, he has helped transform five acres of peat into good farm land—putting in drains to get the water out of the peat, digging up the land to dry it, liming and fertilizing it. His trophies are fields of potatoes, oats, and hay where once nothing except moss could grow.

This croft work is done in Roddy's spare time, and his great dream is more land. He never complains about his double job. What he does say is, "I'd like fine to work the croft all the time, but I'd need more land to make it pay."

Not far away is Neil MacDonald's croft. Though he's away from home eleven hours a day, repairing roads, Mr. MacDonald farms ten acres and has two cows, a few chickens, and some sheep.

"There's no living in a croft," he says regretfully. Then his eyes brighten. "But if I could get hold of a second one—" and his plans pour forth. He'd give up his road work and spend all his time farming. He could raise his own food and some to sell, keep six cows and sell the milk in Portree. More land might mean he could earn a living at the work he likes best, and that is the greatest wealth a crofter like Neil MacDonald wants.

Before Roddy Matheson, Neil MacDonald, and thousands of other land-hungry crofters can get more land, many changes will have to be made. For one thing, the very law passed in 1886 to protect crofters now works against them.

The 1886 law stated that no crofter could be put off his land if he paid his rent. As a result, many crofts are now held by people who do not work them. Some of these people are too old to farm. Some work elsewhere and use their crofts only as places to live. Many crofts have been inherited by people no longer living in the

Highlands. These are the children of crofters, who went away to earn a living and who now hold a croft for vacations or as a place to retire in old age.

Under a new law, the Crofting Commission is trying to make idle land available to men who are willing and able to work it.

With or without more acreage, crofters need help to improve their land. In some places the land is naturally poor. In others it has been ruined by man's misuse.

The felling of forests was a giant blow against the land. Trees hold water in the ground and release it gradually. When trees are stripped from a hillside, rain water runs away over the surface, carrying precious topsoil with it. When trees are stripped from bottom land, rain may turn the ground into a bog. Dead reeds and grasses in the bog decay and become peat in which nothing can be grown.

Overgrazing by sheep also damaged the land. Sheep seek out grass and tender young shoots to eat. They leave alone rough growths such as gorse and bracken. Unless sheep are moved from pasture to pasture, they eat the grass down so far that it cannot reseed itself. In lands where sheep have grazed at will, the coarse growths have taken over. Rooting them out is a tremendous job.

As sheep raising spread in the Highlands, cattle raising fell off. Yet cattle are good for the land. They keep down the coarse growths, eating some and bruising

More cattle would improve the land.

Lauber

others with their hoofs. Cattle droppings fertilize the land, and the cattle themselves work the manure into the soil when their hoofs tear up the ground.

Because of neglect and misuse, once fertile Highland land has gone to waste. If crofting is to be preserved, this land must be brought back into use.

Can it be done?

Oddly, the most dramatic answer has been provided by a man who is neither a crofter nor a farmer. This man is an engineer named John Rollo, a loyal Scot with a deep interest in helping the Highlands. Mr. Rollo has no fondness for the word *can't*. So when defeatists kept saying, "You can't make a ruined croft pay," he decided to prove otherwise.

He read up on crofting while looking around for the worst land he could find in his part of Scotland. Near Easdale, he discovered just what he wanted—an abandoned croft that hadn't been worked in 45 years. Its buildings were ruins. The 10 acres of land were half thin soil, half peat. It was just the sort of place people were calling impossible.

Working by himself and only on week ends, Mr. Rollo proceeded to put the croft back into shape. He built fences, put drains in the peaty land, worked the soil, and constructed buildings. All told, he invested about $1,000 in his croft, plus his own working time. He now has thriving crops of oats, turnips, potatoes, and rye. He has pasture for five head of cattle and grows

John Rollo stands beside the oat crop on his croft. He planted the oats in soil reclaimed from poor, peaty ground.

their winter feed. In a small greenhouse, electrically heated, he produces 500 pounds of tomatoes a year. His profit from these activities is enough to support a small family living simply.

On the island of Lewis, a farm expert named Angus MacLeod has also performed the "impossible." Near North Bragair, he selected a wet, peaty field that was good for nothing. Around it, as far as the eye could see, was more of the same land, so barren that even bracken and rushes could not grow in it. Mr. MacLeod was determined to prove that such land could be improved both easily and cheaply.

With the help of some villagers, he began scattering shell sand and fertilizer over his field. The shell sand was rich in lime to counteract acid in the peat. Seed had been mixed with part of the fertilizer to make sure it would be fertilized where it fell. No plowing was done, and the materials cost less than $30 an acre.

Today, when seen across the hills, that field stands out brilliant green against surrounding land of brown and drab olive. Close up, the contrast is just as great. On one side of a fence is an unimproved field with black peat showing through the thin covering of heather, mosses, and sedge grass. On the other side of the fence is a thick green pasture, sweet with white clover. Beneath the pasture, peat is being turned into good soil as the grass and clover roots circulate air and water through it.

In their experiments, both Mr. Rollo and Mr. MacLeod had certain advantages over the crofters.

Mr. MacLeod had scientific knowledge and good reason to believe his experiment would succeed. Crofters

In foreground is rich pasture planted by Mr. MacLeod. In background is kind of land he reclaimed—useless, moss-covered peat.

Lauber

need to learn new farming methods and they also need leadership. They will learn best if agricultural colleges send more men into the field and set up model crofts.

Mr. Rollo, besides an extraordinary amount of energy, had money to invest in his croft. He could buy supplies and equipment. Crofters can't. They need loans, as well as knowledge, to improve their land.

Mr. Rollo had still one other advantage. There were towns nearby where he could market his food crops.

If crofters are to produce more food, they must have a way of selling it. There is a ready market for croft produce in the Highlands because many towns and hotels must now buy their food from the south. Crofters must have a way to reach that market.

South Uist's egg story is a good example of what can be done.

The old situation was this. On the island of South Uist, crofters' wives raised chickens for eggs. They marketed the eggs by giving them to the man who drove from croft to croft selling groceries. Instead of cash, the housewives were paid in groceries from the truck. Since the housewives knew little about chicken raising, the eggs were of low quality. The grocer couldn't offer much in exchange. So the egg business was poor. Crofters' wives didn't like their payment, and the grocer didn't like the eggs.

This is the new situation. A few years ago, a Scot named Roderick MacFarquhar stepped into the picture.

Lauber

Roderick MacFarquhar, who started South Uist's egg-packing station, poses for photograph with author, Patricia Lauber.

He believed the Highlands could produce top-quality eggs and that both crofters and consumers would benefit. To prove his point, he decided to give up his job and open an egg-packing station on South Uist.

He began by talking to crofters about modern ways of raising chickens and the price good eggs bring. He explained how eggs from 50 or 100 crofts, checked, packed, and sold in big lots could find a mainland market, while 50 or 100 small lots of eggs handled separately could not.

The crofters liked Mr. MacFarquhar's ideas. They got together and raised the money to start an egg-packing station run by Mr. MacFarquhar. From the beginning, the station set a high standard for eggs, paying a good price in cash only for fresh, clean eggs. This made the crofters and their wives eager to learn more about chicken raising and eggs. They began to read up on the subject. From the store that is part of the egg-packing station, they bought better feed, new materials for hen houses, and healthy baby chicks. Within a year, the number of chickens on the island doubled. Quality and quantity of eggs shot upward.

Today eggs are collected from the crofts to be examined, sorted, and packed at the station. The crofters' wives get a report on their eggs and a cash payment with it. And the mainland welcomes the clean, fresh eggs from South Uist. Given an incentive and the chance to make good, crofters' wives have made a successful business out of eggs.

Before South Uist's egg station had been open long, crofters on neighboring islands began to talk about borrowing the idea. By setting the same high standards, they, too, can find good markets. In other parts of the Highlands, egg-packing stations have been in business for years.

The important thing about these stations is that they are co-operatives. A croft is small. Even the best crofts cannot produce many eggs—or potatoes or anything else. Since small crops are hard to sell, crofters must band together and sell their produce in quantity. Only in that way can they find markets.

The same thing is true of buying supplies. It is cheaper to buy in quantity than in small lots. One order for a hundred bales of hay costs less than 20 orders for five bales. This is particularly true in the Highlands, where high freight rates are added to the cost of goods. Only a co-operative can sell jam on South Uist for the same price a Glasgow housewife pays.

Co-operatives have long been running grocery, feed, and supply stores for crofters. But more selling co-operatives are needed if the crofter is to succeed.

More land, better land, and market channels are three of the urgent changes needed in the Highlands, if crofting is to continue as an independent way of life. Still another need is more part-time jobs, for few crofters will ever be able to supply all a family's wants. To earn a decent living, the crofter must have a second job.

What other kinds of jobs can there be? There are several answers to that question, and all of them grow out of the Highlands themselves: out of the sea, the land, the scenery, and even the wet weather.

This trim croft was reclaimed from ruins by hard-working farmer.

Lauber

4. Fishermen Take to the Woods

MEN WHO LIVE by the sea always turn to the sea for food and work. And so the very shape of their country has made Highlanders and Lowlanders alike a sea-minded people, for in Scotland no one is far from the sea.

Scotland is small. It is 274 miles long, while its width varies from 154 miles to 26 miles. But its coastline is 2,300 miles long. The west coast accounts for much of this length. It faces the Atlantic Ocean, and through the ages wind, tide, and waves have worn away land, flooding valleys to form islands and gouging the coast to fringe it with bays and inlets, some of which reach deep into the heart of the mainland. As a result, almost all parts of Scotland are within 40 miles of the sea.

So it has always been natural for Highlanders to turn

toward the sea, to exchange the rocky mountains of the land for the watery mountains of the sea.

For many years, crofters went to sea as fishermen as a way of gaining a cash income. Fishing was a fine second job for them. It did not demand regular hours and could be fitted in around work on the croft. A crofter could fish all day or for only a few hours. If he was going after herring, he fished at night, when darkness helped hide his nets. In winter, when there was no work on the croft, he might sign on a fishing boat going as far away as Iceland or Newfoundland.

Today fishing has been taken over by big, far-ranging boats powered by motor. The crofter can neither afford a big boat nor compete with one. He cannot even work aboard one. The big boats, having taken too many fish from waters close to shore, must go far out to find a catch. This has turned fishing into a full-time job.

Even the full-time fishermen have their troubles. The market for herring, a major Scottish catch, has fallen off badly in the past 40 years.

Until the early 1900's, fishermen sold all the herring they could catch. In Scotland, poor people lived on oatmeal, potatoes, and cheap, nourishing herring. In eastern Europe, there was a good market for pickled or cured herring.

As the standard of living began to rise in this century, people turned away from herring. They wanted, and could pay for, other kinds of fish and meat. Exports

Herring boats moored in Stornoway Bay, Lewis.

British Travel Association

dropped as countries of eastern Europe began to build their own herring fleets.

Highland harbors once packed with herring fleets now have only a few boats. The Shetland herring fleet decreased from 785 boats in 1913 to 50 in 1953. Stornoway, on the island of Lewis, used to have a fleet of 60 boats. Now it has 10 or 12.

The shrinking herring market has also cut back shore jobs in pickling and curing. A large part of each catch is preserved because fresh herring are so rich in oil that they go bad rapidly. The bigger the demand for herring, the more shore jobs there are.

Pickling is done by women working in open sheds along the waterfront. While seagulls cry and swoop overhead, looking for tidbits, women clean and gut the fish, dip them in coarse salt, and pack them in barrels.

Curing is done indoors. Cleaned and gutted fish are placed in ovens on the top floor of the factory. There they are cured in smoke rising from a slow fire of oak chips far below.

When the herring industry was booming, many men and women were employed at pickling and curing the fish or making the barrels and cases in which preserved herring were shipped. Today only a fraction of those workers are needed. Some others work in quick-freezing plants or in factories where oil is taken from herring for fertilizer and fish are turned into meal for animal feed. But unless scientists find more new uses for herring, the

Cleaned, gutted herring are dipped in salt, packed in barrels.

industry cannot offer many jobs to crofters or other Highlanders.

Today the most successful crofter-fishermen are lobstermen.

Lobsters abound in the rocky shallows of west Scotland's ragged coast. They are caught in traps, which look like a basket with a funnel-shaped opening. Lured by the fish bait, a lobster explores the opening and, once inside, can't get out again.

A lobster fisherman lowers his traps to the bottom and marks their position with floats. Then he leaves them and goes home, returning sometime later to haul up the traps and remove the lobsters. This kind of work goes well with crofting.

Western Scotland has always had lobsters, but in earlier days marketing problems discouraged crofters from trapping them. Most lobstering was done in summer, when the seas were calm. This meant that all lobsters arrived at market in the same season and their number drove the price down. It also meant that many lobsters died during the slow trip south in warm weather, even though they were packed in ice. Since dead shellfish rapidly go bad, crofters were not paid for those that died. All told, lobstering was not very profitable.

Now a co-operative with modern marketing methods has made lobstering such good business that three quarters of all crofter-fishermen are lobstermen.

The fisherman sells his lobsters directly to the co-operative. He doesn't have to bother with shipping them or worrying over the number that may die during the trip.

By keeping lobsters alive in pounds of fresh sea water, the co-operative has a year-round supply. If lobsters are plentiful in the market, the co-operative holds back its lobsters until the price is better.

The biggest pound is at Oban, a west-coast port with good transportation. This pound is not only a storehouse for lobsters but also a resting place. Lobsters from the far north are unpacked at Oban and turned loose in the pound to refresh themselves. After a couple of days, they are repacked in ice and sent on, as fresh and lively as if they had just been caught.

Lobsters are promising and they will support some of the men who used to be crofter-fishermen. What is to become of the others?

Fortunately, a new occupation is opening up to take the place of fishing. This is forestry. Yesterday's crofter doubled as a fisherman. Tomorrow's crofter will take to the woods and double as a lumberman. The greatest and best hope for the future of the Highlands lies not in the sea but in forests.

The forests are new ones. Two and a half million acres of trees are being planted in Scotland, a large proportion of them in the Highlands. Hundreds of Highlanders are already at work raising trees from seeds, planting young trees and caring for them. In time, when the trees mature, forests will provide tens of thousands of jobs. Many men will find work in forest care. Four times as many will work for companies leasing timber rights, felling trees, hauling them out, manning sawmills, and working in industries using wood.

The first effects of these forests can already be seen. Where there are forest jobs, villages spring to life—new houses are built, schools reopen, churches fill, shops bustle, and roads go through. The effects are felt far out into the countryside, where crofters and shepherds are no longer isolated but within reach of a living village.

Equally important, these forests, coupled with others in England and Wales, will give Britain a timber reserve, something the country has long lacked.

The felling of Scotland's forests began with the

Women are lifting seedling spruce from nursery for planting.

Vikings and continued for a thousand years, into modern times. People burned forests to get rid of the wolves and robber bands that hid in them. In the 1700's, forest after forest fell to make charcoal for smelting iron ore. Later, other forests were burned to open up land for sheep. Some planting was done to beautify large estates. But on the whole the history of Scotland's forests is one of destruction, capped by two world wars in which Britain, cut off from foreign timber supplies, had to sacrifice many of its remaining forests.

To create timberlands, government foresters in 1946 began planting five million acres of trees, half of them in Scotland. The planting reached its peak in Scotland during 1954. In that one year, 53 million trees were planted on 34,344 acres of new forest, while another six million replacements went into the ground.

Even in the open Highlands, it's impossible to plant all these acres of forests without taking land that some people think should be used for sheep or farming. The land that farmers can't use—wind-swept, rocky hilltops and sodden peat bogs—will not grow trees either. A tree must have soil in which to plant its roots firmly.

Some farm land, though not the best, has been sacrificed to forests, but in return trees improve the land near them. They keep topsoil from being washed away. Their leaves or needles decaying on the ground add richness to the soil. Crops sheltered from the wind by trees grow better, ripen sooner, and are less likely to be killed by cold.

In protected pastures, grass grows thicker and comes up earlier in the spring. Sheep and cattle sheltered from the wind require less food to keep themselves warm. Trees may take land from grazing, but the remaining pasture can support more animals than it could before.

Team of men is planting seedlings on barren Highland hillside.

Forestry Commission

Good farm land has been planted with tree breaks for shelter.

In fact, the number of sheep in Scotland has increased since the forest planting started.

In a roundabout way, forests even solve one of the major problems in sheep raising—getting shepherds. These days, few men wish to live in the wilds of a sheep range where their wives are lonely and the future offers no jobs for their children. If there's a forest nearby, this picture changes. Where there's a forest, there's a village of workers—a school, a church, shops, amusements, people to visit. Where there's a forest, there are jobs for young people and a reason for them to stay home.

Perhaps most important of all—acre for acre, forests can support more people than sheep raising can. Only 2 or 3 men are needed to care for sheep on 1,000 acres.

But 15 men are needed to plant and care for trees on this same amount of land. As planting ends, this number drops, but it rises still higher when the young trees are big enough to require thinning. When the trees mature in another 60 or so years, sawmills, pulp mills, and other wood industries will move into the Highlands. At that time, 1,000 acres of trees will supply jobs for 75 men on full time, or several times that number on part time.

To date, the northern and western Highland sea-

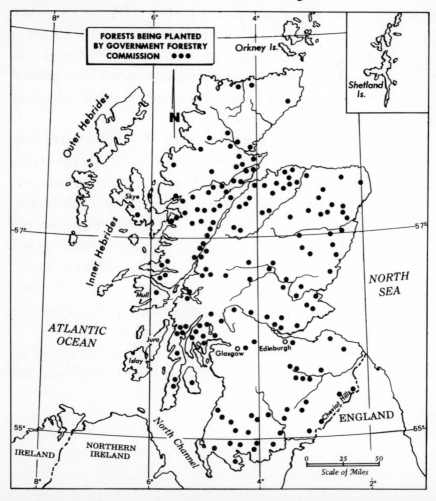

boards remain almost completely unforested, though that is the region most in need of help. The reasons for this are several.

First of all, there is the land. Some of it is impossible to plant. Rock is too close to the surface, the ocean wind too strong, or the land too peaty. In other places, trees could be planted in the peat, but no one knows how long or how big they would grow or whether, with their roots in peat, they could survive gale storms.

Secondly, there was the problem of getting workers. Outside workers refused to go to the northwest, saying it was too rainy and too far from civilization. Local crofters, struggling to survive in a barren land, refused to co-operate. Forests, they thought, would take over what little farm land they had.

Now the crofters know better. They have heard how forests help the land and provide jobs. They know that forests, crofting, sheep, and cattle can survive together.

But some of the men in charge of forestry still hesitate to start planting the northwest coasts. "Have we the right," they ask, "to spend the taxpayers' money planting trees where we are not sure they will grow well?"

Others answer that the risk must be taken. The planting of forests is the chief long-term hope for saving the Highlands. Every region must be given its chance.

Where there are forests, new villages will spring up and old ones come to life, for forests mean jobs and jobs mean people.

5. From Tourists to Seaweed

Young, green forests taking root in the Highlands hold out a shining promise for the future. While foresters continue the tree planting, other men are tackling Highland job problems of today and next year. They are trying to make sure there will be enough jobs to hold Highlanders until the trees mature.

In some cases these men are trying to expand traditional industries so as to create more or better jobs. In other cases they're trying to create new industries—and new jobs. Both old and new jobs are needed. If they develop quickly enough, they will bridge the gap between today and the forest-filled future.

1. Traditional Jobs

One booming Highland business is the tourist trade. Every summer thousands of visitors pour into the Highlands. Some have come to hunt or fish. Most are there to enjoy Highland scenery of rolling mountains, sky-blue lakes, blankets of purple heather, crystal streams, and cliff-lined bays.

In the Highlands, as in all countries with scenery to sell, taking care of the tourists is big business. During summer, hotels are filled to bursting point, and many crofting families find jobs in them.

These jobs—like the tourist season itself—would be better if they lasted longer. Visitors pour into the Highlands only during the two or three summer months. There are so few tourists at other times of year that hotels stand empty and locked for nine or ten months. Yet in summer there's scarcely a bed to be had in the Highlands by three or four in the afternoon, and hotels must turn away visitors who have no reservations.

The Scottish Tourist Board would like to see many more visitors in the Highlands, for tourism is a major source of income. How could the Highlands handle more tourists? The Board has two answers which would help both visitors and Highlanders.

The immediate solution is to make more beds available, and the Board is doing this in a novel way. In town after town, village after village, it seeks out families who will put up overnight guests, and then lists their names and addresses for tourists. In this way, tourists get a place to sleep and a chance to meet the people of the country they are visiting. Highland families earn a good, steady income during the summer months.

The long-range solution is to persuade visitors that summer isn't the only season for enjoying Highland scenery, that spring and fall are also lovely. If the tourist season can be extended, hotels will gain more business and will stay open longer. The longer hotels stay open, the better jobs crofting families will find in them. Five or six months of steady wages would be a good supplement to crofting income and make it possible for young people to earn a decent living in the Highlands.

The tourist trade is a fairly widespread Highland industry, but most of it is found on the mainland and on the near-lying, lovely Isle of Skye. On the distant, wind-swept islands of the Outer Hebrides and the far north, where few tourists ever go, the people have developed specialties of their own.

Highland games—contests of strength and skill—are big tourist attractions wherever they are held.   British Travel Association

On the Shetland Islands, off the northern tip of Scotland, the women are famed for their knitting. Using ancient patterns and soft wool from Shetland sheep, about 6,000 women and girls—almost the whole female population—earn money by knitting goods that are sold all over the world. In the Shetlands, crofting, fishing, and knitting support most of the people.

In the Outer Hebrides weaving is the specialty and an ancient skill.

Weaving started long ago as a home skill on the crofts. When the men of the family sheared their sheep, the women took the wool, cleaned, dyed, carded, and spun it, then wove it into cloth. Much of the cloth was a heavy tweed.

In the late 1800's, this tweed caught the attention of wealthy sportsmen hunting and fishing in the Highlands. It stood up well under hard wear; its heavy weight kept the wearer warm in winter, while its loose weave made it suitable for summer. The sportsmen started buying tweed from crofters, taking it home, and having their tailors make it up into jackets, trousers, and caps. Soon other people began wanting this tweed, too. And that was the start of weaving as an island industry. The tweed itself was named for Harris, one of the islands on which it was made.

Today six million yards of Harris Tweed are sold every year, a third of them in the United States alone. The orders are handled by big mills, which process the

Some older people, like this spinner, still prepare their own wool.

Lauber

wool to make sure quality and colors are uniform. But the weaving is still done by crofters working on hand looms in their own homes.

Lewis and Harris have many crofter-weaver villages. Walking through one, you soon become aware of a strange noise—*click, click, clank.* That is the sound of the loom. In a shed near the house, the crofter sits before his loom on a high bench. His feet work pedals that adjust the warp threads to form the pattern. The shuttle shoots back and forth between his hands, ending with a *click* on each side. The *clank* comes as the weaver pulls the threads tight.

The crofter's wool comes from a mill and the woven tweed goes back to the mill, but the crofter remains his own master. He sets his own hours and spends as much —or as little—time as he wishes weaving. He is paid by the finished tweed, not by the hour. Weaving is one of the best jobs that can be coupled with crofting.

For that reason, Harris Tweed has become a "protected industry." Nothing may be called Harris Tweed unless it is made from Scottish wool—spun, dyed, and finished in the Outer Hebrides, and hand-woven by islanders in their own homes. This Board of Trade ruling protects the industry against machine-made imitations. Harris Tweed is a crofter industry. On some islands it has preserved crofting as a way of life. The big demand for Harris Tweed occurred just after the island fishing industry failed. So crofter-fishermen became crofter-weavers. Thanks to tweed, the crofters could stay home and earn their living with an ancient skill highly prized by the modern world.

Crofter-weaver works in stone shed beside his house.

Harris Tweed Association

2. New Industries

In all the Highlands, there is only one big industry
—the British Aluminum Company. British Aluminum
moved into the Highlands during the early 1900's,
attracted by rushing mountain streams. These streams
promised plentiful water power for making the electricity required to produce aluminum. Today the company has three plants at Fort William, Kinlochleven,
and Foyers. It has bought up huge tracts of land in these
regions to protect its watersheds. And it is planting
thousands of trees on this land. The trees will one day
be valuable timber. Meanwhile, they hold water in the
soil and gradually release it, insuring a steady supply
of water.

Some people think that more big industries would
solve Highland problems, but this is not so. For the
most part, the Highland people are scattered over the
land. There are no large population centers to form a
pool of factory labor. And if people were drawn off the
land into factory towns, that would destroy crofting
as a way of life.

If there are to be Highland factories, they must be
small ones, employing only a few men. Such factories
could well save the Highlands. Their jobs and steady
wages would hold young people without destroying
crofting.

Are small factories possible? Ten or fifteen years ago,

most people found the idea laughable. "Highlanders have no industrial skills," they said. "Anyway, small factories aren't profitable." Today those people have had to change their thinking. They've been proved wrong by John Rollo, the same man who made a success out of a ruined croft.

Mr. Rollo believed that crofting could be combined with light industry *if* the factory employed only a few men and *if* its work was arranged so that the men could take time off for planting or harvesting.

Ignoring the skeptics, Mr. Rollo tried putting his ideas into practice. In 1940 he took over an old smithy at Easdale and opened a small factory to make parts for his main factory in Scotland's industrial belt. In the beginning, one man and a boy helper staffed the factory. But with the wartime need for machine tools, the work

New small industries are needed to supplement traditional jobs such as sheep raising. These sheep are raised for their wool.

Harris Tweed Association

force swelled to 12 men and 2 women. Since the war, the Easdale factory has continued in high gear, and what a difference it has made!

In 1940, Easdale, with little crofting and no industry, was losing its young people and in danger of being abandoned. Today Easdale, thanks to its tiny factory, is a small but thriving community.

In 1951, encouraged by Easdale, Mr. Rollo opened another small factory at Inverasdale, 200 miles farther north. Six crofters, working in an old army hut, learned mechanical skills by producing half a million bolts to be used in the foundations of big oil refineries. Then they advanced to assembling little tractors, designed by Mr. Rollo for use on crofts. The assembly work was arranged so that if one man needed time off for his croft, the others could continue without him.

Steady wages for six men have made a big difference in Inverasdale.

In 1956, Inverasdale's school population rose from 12 to 15, as the factory workers' children reached school age. This was the first time in 40 years that the number of schoolchildren had increased instead of decreased.

Jack MacLean, the young foreman, says, "It would be impossible to stay here without this factory. If there were only more jobs like this, a lot of men who've gone away would come back."

The oldest employee, John MacPherson, adds, "If we'd had work like this earlier, we'd have kept our children home."

In 1953, Mr. Rollo opened a third factory at Wick, in the most northerly part of the Highlands. Employing six men, it makes iron castings—manhole covers, supports for park benches, and parts for the tractors assembled at Inverasdale. It is the only foundry in the Highlands.

Since Highland freight charges are very expensive, Mr. Rollo uses his own trucks to transport the heavy products of his northern factories. Factories making light objects would not need their own transportation.

If other manufacturers follow Mr. Rollo's lead, crofting communities will take a new lease on life. But the benefits will by no means be one-sided. Highlanders are quick learners and good workers. The result is small factories showing a clear profit.

Tiny Rollo factory enables these men to stay in Inverasdale.

Lauber

3. New Resources

Natural resources act as a magnet to attract industry. In many parts of the world, undeveloped regions have suddenly sprung to life when important resources were found in them. Could this happen in the Highlands? Perhaps—no one really knows. In modern times no thorough search has been made to find out if resources lie hidden in Highland mountains, glens, and waters.

Known resources are few. The greatest of them is water. Water power attracted British Aluminum. Water with an odd peaty taste goes into Scotch whisky and accounts for the distinctive flavor. The purity of Highland water may someday draw the chemical industry north. The Highlands also have slate and limestone, and in time they will offer timber.

Those resources alone cannot save the Highlands. Their chief hope lies in the discovery of strange resources for which modern industry and science have found uses that no one even dreamed of 50 years ago. The experiments of white-coated scientists in far-away laboratories have already created jobs for several hundred crofters who are tapping two odd but important Highland resources.

One was first discovered by accident many years ago. In the early 1800's, a duck hunter waded out of Loch (Lake) Cuithir on Skye and noticed that his legs were covered with white stuff. Being curious, he scraped some off and sent it away to be analyzed. The answer came back that the white material was diatomite.

Diatoms are tiny, one-celled water plants. Diatomite is the fossil remains of these plants—the cell walls or skeletons. Each skeleton is many-sided, hollow, and light in weight.

At the time diatomite was discovered on Skye, nobody wanted it. In the late 1800's, manufacturers began using it as insulation and as filler in dynamite. From 1890 to 1913, the loch was worked on a small scale.

Today industry has found so many uses for diatomite that it is in great demand. Since Loch Cuithir holds the largest known deposit in Great Britain, it is being steadily worked. The mining and processing of diatomite employs 65 men on Skye for at least half the year.

At the drained loch, steamshovels gouge out diatomite, which looks like clay. When first dug, the hollow cells of the diatomite are full of water. Trucks carry the material away and dump it for 10 days of open-air

Lauber

Manager of Skye plant stands beside diatomite drying in the open air.

drying. That removes about half the water. The rest vanishes in the furnaces of the processing plant at Uig. There the diatomite is also crushed into soft, white powder, packed in bags, and shipped to manufacturers in big cities.

Diatomite goes into many products. Because it is strong but light, it is sometimes mixed with concrete to lessen the weight. Because it is silky smooth, diatomite goes into face powder and talcum powder. Because it won't burn, it goes into fire-proof boarding. Because of its hollow structure, diatomite makes a fine filter for oils, fruit juices, beer, and waxes.

Those are just some of the uses industry has found for the "white stuff" of Loch Cuithir. But the list is short compared with the uses industry has found for the second odd Highland resource—seaweed.

From certain kinds of seaweed, scientists can extract substances called alginates. (The name comes from algae, the family of plants to which seaweed belongs.) Chiefly since the end of World War II, U. S. and British scientists have found hundreds of uses for alginates and are still discovering new ones. Without knowing it, most of us are eating or using alginates every day in the year.

Here are just a few of the products alginates go into:

An alginate that thickens other substances is used in making sauces, soups, cream fillings, toothpaste, hand creams, ointments, lotions, liquid detergents.

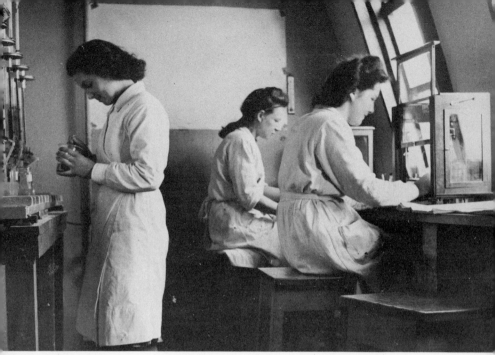

Alginate Industries Ltd.

In lab near Oban technicians extract alginates from seaweed.

Another alginate is a stabilizer. That is, it keeps various other ingredients from separating. This one is used in ice cream, soft drinks, car wax and other polishes, insect sprays.

A third alginate, which helps jelling, goes into puddings, custards, jellies, and the material a dentist uses to make an impression of your teeth.

A fourth alginate is used to make filmlike coatings and threads. It turns up in sausage casings that can be eaten, transparent paper, coated papers, and washable wallpaper. This alginate is also a soluble, which means it dissolves in liquid. For that reason it is used to make a new kind of surgical dressing. If this dressing is left

Crofters work with Tangles of the Isles on the beach.

in a wound, the doctor doesn't have to reopen the wound to get it out. After a few days, when the dressing has done its work, it dissolves and is absorbed into the blood stream.

The same alginate has many uses in the textile industry. For example, alginate threads can be twisted into very fine wool to strengthen it against the strain of weaving. When the weaving is finished, the alginate threads are dissolved in water, leaving only the fine fabric of soft wool.

Movie and TV producers have an odd use for this alginate. If the script calls for someone to be shot, they may dress him in a shirt made of alginate threads. The victim is "shot" with water. The "bullet hole" shown by the camera is actually the spot where water dissolved the shirt.

The many uses for alginates have caused a boom in

harvesting certain kinds of seaweed. Off California, giant kelp is harvested by machine. In Ireland and northwest Scotland, where rocky coasts rule out machines, crofters do the work by hand.

On South Uist, one of the main Highland seaweed centers, winter gales over the Atlantic wash ashore huge masses of seaweed. It is the kind we call kelp, but its local name is Tangles of the Isles. Crofters pick up the seaweed and break off the frond, which is the leafy end. Since fronds have no value for alginates, the people take these home and use them for fertilizer. The stems are spread out to dry, then sold to the South Uist mill where they are dried further in ovens, ground to powder, and

Air-dryed Tangle stems are collected and taken to mill.

Alginate Industries Ltd.

At South Uist mill seaweed is oven dried, ground, and bagged.

bagged. The powder is sent to a factory in Oban where the alginates are extracted.

In summer, when the sea is quiet, crofters collect rockweed, which they cut from the rocks with a sickle at low tide. As the tide begins to come in, the cut seaweed is pulled ashore in floats by long ropes.

Years ago crofters earned a good living collecting and burning seaweed for soap. When that industry collapsed, their only use for this gift of the sea was on the croft, where it became fertilizer or animal feed. Today, thanks to modern science, there is a big and good market for seaweed that brings a cash income to several hundred crofters.

Perhaps a modern survey would show that the Highlands have other odd resources for which today's world has found a use. If so, there is no telling what kind of jobs might open up for the Highland people.

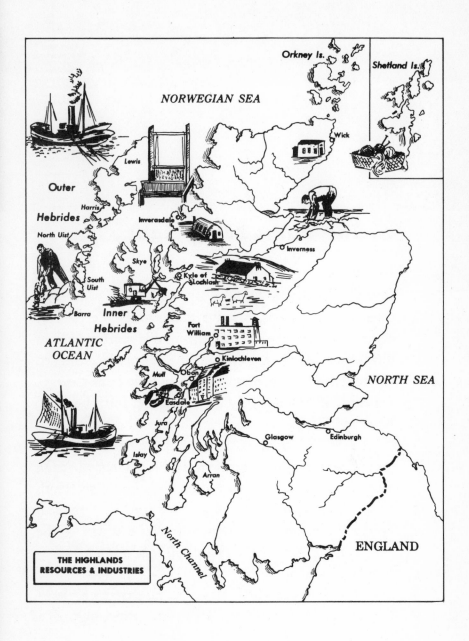

NORWEGIAN SEA

Orkney Is.

Shetland Is.

Wick

Outer

Hebrides

Lewis

Harris

North Uist

Inverasdale

Inverness

South
Uist

Skye

Barra

Inner

Hebrides

ATLANTIC
OCEAN

Kyle of
Lochlash

Fort
William

Kinlochleven

Mull   Oban

Easdale

Jura

Islay

Arran

Glasgow   Edinburgh

NORTH SEA

North Channel

ENGLAND

THE HIGHLANDS
RESOURCES & INDUSTRIES

6. The Rains Bring Light

KYLE OF LOCHALSH consists of a big hotel, a handful of houses, a few shops. Massive mountains tower behind the village. On the sea side, beyond a narrow arm of blue water, lies Skye, its mountains alternately curtained and revealed by the mists. Two busy little ferries, carrying cars and passengers, scurry back and forth between Kyle and Skye.

That is just about all that the thousands of summer visitors who pass through Kyle ever see. Only the most sharp-eyed notice a small, neat building on the road into Kyle. Made of native stone and screened by trees and shrubs, the building is easy to miss. Yet it is part of the most exciting story in the Highlands today. It is a hydro-electric power plant.

Until a few years ago, no home, no shop in Kyle of Lochalsh had electricity. Then, the throwing of a

This is all there is to be seen of the Lochalsh power plant.

switch in the newly completed power plant brought the village into the twentieth century. Electric lights, radios, and irons were no longer just pictures seen in magazines. Overnight they became realities, things people could own and use in their homes.

On the main street there's a small electric appliance shop. To outsiders, its wares are commonplace. To the local people they represent a whole new world. And this same new world is opening up all over the Highlands today.

Torquil Nicolson, manager of the power plant, has his office back of the shop. Himself a dynamo of energy, Mr. Nicolson is a hard man to catch, but once found he proudly whisks an interested visitor up the mountain to a loch, as a Scottish lake is called. This loch, fed by streams and drainage from surrounding mountains, is the reservoir of water power. A dam releases water into a huge tube running down the mountainside in a breath-taking drop. At the other end of the tube is the power house. The water, gathering tremendous force as it drops, powers the turbines below that spin the generators that produce electricity.

Inside the trim power house, all that can be seen is a bewildering array of gauges and switches and the massive, gleaming machines that produce electricity. Outside, there is no smoke, no noise, nothing to draw attention to the small plant that has brought modern ways to Kyle, neighboring villages, and outlying crofts. Even the great tube on the mountainside is hidden by trees and shrubs.

With a glance at his watch, Mr. Nicolson suggests a quick trip to nearby Plockton, his own village. There in a hilltop barn is an experimental hay drier, made possible by the coming of electricity.

Grass, Mr. Nicolson explains, grows green and thick in the damp climate of the Highlands. But the same rain makes cutting and drying hay a risky business, for wet hay rots. With an electric drier, the farmer is no longer at the weather's mercy. Rain or shine, his hay dries quickly.

Since no crofter could afford his own hay drier, the Plockton one is run as a co-operative, setting an example that may be followed all over the Highlands.

In a field beside the drier, a fine potato crop grows. This is one of Mr. Nicolson's own experiments. The field was once peaty ground, good for little. By way of showing local crofters what could be done, Mr. Nicolson drained it, plowed it, added lime and fertilizer, then planted it. He sells his potatoes to a local hotel. "Crofters need to be encouraged and shown the way," he says. "They've been neglected so long that they've lost heart."

On the way back to Kyle, Mr. Nicolson confides that he's thinking of opening a small boatyard at Plockton now that there's electricity for power tools. "Just a few men with steady wages would make a big difference here," he says.

Setting an example for crofters and starting a boat-yard in his spare time is not at all unusual for a man like

An electric hay drier offsets the damp climate of the Highlands.

North of Scotland Hydro-Electric Board

Torquil Nicolson. First, like John Rollo and Roderick MacFarquhar, he's a man determined to help the Highlands. Second, Mr. Nicolson works for the North of Scotland Hydro-Electric Board, and there is never any telling what the Board's men will start next.

The Hydro Board, which has been at work since the 1940's, has two assignments. One is to produce cheap electricity for the Highlands. The other is to improve living conditions any way it can. This second assignment has involved the Hydro Board in everything from developing electric hay driers to breeding fish.

Basically the Hydro Board is tapping the Highlands' greatest resource—running water. The Highlands have more water power than any other part of Britain. This is why:

The world's prevailing winds come from the west. As these winds sweep across the Atlantic Ocean, they become heavy with moisture. On reaching northwest Scotland, the water-heavy winds strike the mountain tops. Because the mountain air is colder than the wind, it causes the moisture to condense and fall as rain. The rain feeds countless streams that rush down mountains and hills. The streams run into lochs.

Many of these lochs are several hundred feet above sea level. Their water, in turn, runs off to lower bodies of water. By harnessing the run-off from high lochs, engineers can use the water power to produce electricity. In this way the heavy rains and great green mountains bring light to the Highlands.

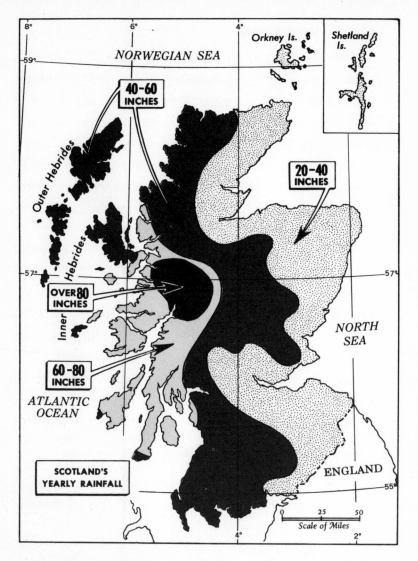

NORWEGIAN SEA

Orkney Is.

Shetland Is.

8°   6°   4°

59°

40-60 INCHES

Outer Hebrides

20-40 INCHES

57°   57°

OVER 80 INCHES

Inner Hebrides

NORTH SEA

60-80 INCHES

ATLANTIC OCEAN

SCOTLAND'S YEARLY RAINFALL

ENGLAND

55°

0   25   50
Scale of Miles

4°   2°

By late 1956, the Hydro Board had 25 power plants in operation, 17 under construction, and 16 in the planning stage. About 60 per cent of the farms and crofts in the Highlands were receiving electricity, and 16,000 new consumers were tapping in each year. In 1948 only

1 farm out of 14 and 1 croft out of 100 had electricity.

What a difference the coming of electricity has made! On a lonely croft electric lights replace oil lamps; a radio brightens long winter evenings; an electric heater warms corners away from the fire. In crofts and villages, housewives can have electric stoves, kettles, irons, washing machines, refrigerators, vacuum cleaners, hot-water heaters, sewing machines, toasters. Even the dentist can have an electric drill.

Until a few years ago, the crofter's wife not only did the cooking, cleaning, mending, milking, feeding of livestock (as well as giving a hand with the field work), but did all this without the help of electricity. In addition, she had to carry all water from the village well or perhaps from a loch half a mile away. Faced with a life of unending drudgery, it is small wonder that Highland girls left in droves for other parts of the world.

Today Highlanders are finally getting conveniences

An electric stove is delivered to a crofter's thatched house.

North of Scotland Hydro-Electric Board

North of Scotland Hydro-Electric Board

Electrically heated brooders keep chicks warm and comfortable.

the rest of us take for granted. The government is laying water mains to supply running water. The Hydro Board is stringing lines that will carry electricity to all who want it.

The same electricity that makes life pleasanter for the crofter's wife helps her husband produce more food.

Electricity means more eggs. Hens lay eggs only when it is light. With electricity, a crofter can light the hen house and lengthen short winter days.

Infra-red light keeps baby pigs warm and prevents them from smothering one another in a struggle to get next to the sow. Here electricity means more pigs.

If co-operative hay driers spread through the Highlands, crofters will be sure of their crop. The hay will be more nourishing. Quick electric drying leaves the hay a higher protein value than slow open-air drying. Better hay means cows produce more milk, steers gain more weight.

Electricity also means opportunity for men with ideas. In the short time that some villages have had electricity, many new jobs have opened up. With power-driven tools, garages and blacksmith shops can make repairs on cars, buses, and farm machinery that used to be sent south. One man has started a refrigerating plant for white heather, which many Highlanders consider lucky for weddings. Another has opened a boatyard. Men are using electricity to can fruit, quick-freeze fish, spin flax, and power tools for making furniture. Electricity made possible John Rollo's small factories. It made possible the diatomite processing plant on Skye.

The Hydro Board even creates jobs itself. It uses local labor for construction. By insisting on local stone for its buildings, instead of brick from the south, the Board revived Highland quarrying. It has coaxed several manufacturers to open small plants in the Highlands. Certain companies manufacturing electrical supplies sell their goods to the Hydro Board. So the Board suggested that these companies open Highland branches. Up to this time, manufacturers had avoided the Highlands, saying there was no power, no trained labor, no market at hand. The Hydro Board said, "Now there's power. We are your market. And we're sure you'll find workers who are quick to learn."

Power tools, like this sander, help small industries in the Highlands.

Much metal work formerly had to be sent out of the Highlands.

BIRNAM DUNKELD

APPROACH TO THE HIGHLANDS

Clunie Dam on the River Tummel blends into the lovely scenery.

One company that decided to give the Highlands a try took over an old tweed mill and opened a small factory to make electric meters. It found Highland workers quick and intelligent. The pure, clean Highland air dropped no soot into delicate mechanisms. The company was so pleased that it recently expanded the Highland plant to handle big new orders from South America.

The only people who feared the coming of electricity were vacationers. They were afraid the Hydro Board's work would destroy the scenery and ruin the fishing.

But if anything, the Board has made the Highlands better for tourists.

Formerly hotels had to generate their own electricity. Now they can buy large quantities of cheap power and install all the kitchen appliances they want. In addition, with electricity (and running water) many private homes can now take in overnight guests. The villagers earn more money, and more beds are available for tourists.

Since it had to tamper with lochs and rivers, the Hydro Board decided to improve fishing. It bred fish, stocked waters with them, removed killer fish, and built fish passes so that salmon going upstream could get by obstructions. A glass-enclosed fish pass at Pitlochery has turned out to be a big tourist attraction.

Pitlochery fish pass (on either side of road) is tourist attraction.

North of Scotland Hydro-Electric Board

In many areas the Hydro Board has built the first roads.

As for scenery, the Board's men try to put it back the way they found it. Trees and bushes hide pipelines and power plants.

To put up power lines, the Board had to build roads. Wherever possible, it zigzagged the roads to make them pass by outlying crofts and give crofters a route into town. Tourists, of course, are also free to use the roads.

Although the Board hides its construction, many visitors seek out the dams and power plants because they like to see how these things work. Visitors from under-

North of Scotland Hydro-Electric Board

Dams and power stations interest many foreign visitors from under-developed countries. Dam shown lies in the mountains above Kyle of Lochalsh. Below: the dam's generating station.

North of Scotland Hydro-Electric Board

This special tractor is harvesting peat to be used in Board's gas turbines. Stripped land will be good for farming, forests.

developed countries are interested in the way electricity has been brought to the Highlands through a series of small dams and power plants. For these visitors, the Highlands are a show window of British engineering skill.

As if this weren't enough, the Board is experimenting with other kinds of power. On the windy Orkney Islands, it is trying windmills as a way of producing electricity. At Caithness, on the northern tip of the mainland, Board men are drying and pulverizing peat. The peat is used to fuel a gas turbine in the production of electricity. In that part of the country, peat overlies good soil. So cutting peat both provides power and reclaims land.

At Dounreay there's an atomic reactor, scheduled to produce electricity by 1958. The Board welcomes atomic power as a friend, not a competitor, saying, "There's need for all kinds of power in the Highlands."

And so there is.

Plentiful electricity, making possible new industry, new opportunity, and comfortable homes, holds out one of the brightest hopes for the Highlands' future. The coming of electricity represents a great victory in the battle of the Highlands. At long last progress is making itself felt in northwest Scotland and bringing modern conveniences into the people's lives. No longer need young people leave home to enjoy the pleasure of flipping a switch for light. No longer need a man be forced to live as his great-grandfather did.

New forests are another victory. In time to come, timberlands will offer steady work to thousands upon thousands of men. Forests promise better times ahead than the Highlands have ever known.

Where there are forests, new villages spring up.

Elsewhere on the battleground there are encouraging signs. Task forces on trial runs have proved that small factories can help the Highlands and show a profit for their owners. They have proved that resources do exist. They have proved there is a demand not only for High-

Once ruined land can be reclaimed to support herds of cattle.

Hobbs Ranch, Inverlochy Castle

land scenery but also for Highland skills. Above all else they have proved that crofting *can* be made to pay.

A handful of determined men have proved the doubting Thomases wrong. They have shown that Highland problems can be solved.

What is needed now are massive follow-up attacks. The attacks must come quickly, for time is growing short. They must be made with every weapon available, for the problem is deep-rooted and the prize is great.

The future of the Highlands hangs on these attacks. They, and they alone, will determine whether the piper is to play a sad and final lament for the Highlands or whether his tune is to be a joyous celebration of good times and a welcome home to those who have gone away.

Sheep graze at the foot of Ben Nevis, as they have for many years. Above them slender wires carrying electricity bring new ways and opportunity to the ancient Scottish Highlands.

Index